# Psychic
# Made
# Super Simple

## Beginner Basics of
## Psychic Development
## & Workbook

Aerin Kube, Ph.D

ISBN: 9798678774422

Library of Congress Control Number: 2020916563

Printed in the United States of America.

First printing edition 2020.

www.aerinkube.com

# Dedication

*To God, the angels, my husband, my children, and my family. This book is dedicated to you for your love and support. Special thanks to my friends, teachers, and the spiritual community.*

# About the Author

Aerin Kube is a mom of six, an Author, Parapsychologist, Teacher, and Psychic Medium. She earned a Ph.D in Metaphysics and Parapsychology from the University of Metaphysical Sciences, a non-secular college in California, accredited by the American Alternative Medical Association and the American Association Of Drugless Practitioners. She has also trained under many renowned spiritual leaders.

Before the unfoldment of her spiritual journey, she worked in corporate America. Having attended secular colleges and universities she received degrees in business and liberal arts.

Her knowledge and strengths come from her experience in teaching, writing, counseling, real estate, marketing, theater, and public speaking, as well as her past as a successful entrepreneur of a renowned multi-location operation for expectant families around Michigan.

Ordained, she holds certifications in Reiki, IET, life coaching, and mediumship. Her passion is psychical studies, philosophy, and helping others see the light within them.

# Table of Contents

# Welcome to Your
# New Spiritual Journey

If you are reading this book, then you are on the right track. You are discovering that you are psychic and have come to a point in your life where you want your questions answered.

Welcome to the start of your new spiritual journey towards understanding your soul better. I'm so glad you are here and that I can help you on your path.

This book was designed to be short and sweet. It is only to provide you with some simple and basic information to get you started. Know that there is a wealth of information out there for you to learn when you are ready.

# Chapter 1

# What Is A Psychic

Getting started, let me share with you that you have had the God-given gifts of being psychic since birth and even before that. We are all naturally psychic, but most of us don't use the term or acknowledge it. If you are brand new and have been feeling confused or overwhelmed, then know you are not alone.

Working with students, I've found they all come in with different feelings. Some people seem shaken and scared, some are anxious, and overwhelmed, while some are delighted and excited. Whatever you are feeling, realize there are others just like you. However, no one is exactly like you. You may have heard that sentiment since grade school, but I'm here to tell you that it applies to your psychic abilities too. It's been my experience that everyone's skills are all unique.

The first thing I want to do is ask a question. When describing a psychic person, how do you perceive them? Are you seeing them as special people, frauds, supernatural, or everyday people? The answer to this should be ordinary people because everyone is psychic!

## *How Do You Perceive Psychics?*

_____

_____

_____

_____

_____

_____

_____

_____

# Chapter 2

# Where Does Information

# Come From

About now, you might be asking where all this inner knowledge is coming from and why. Well, let's make it quick and easy. Everything in the universe is made of energy. We are energy, and we can read this energy because the information is around us, and it's always moving.

We can use our sixth sense to receive information by allowing images, impressions, and feelings to come in. When our mind is quiet and relaxed, then we can tap in and read that energy easier. Consider it a gift from the universe or your Creator, God, and a Divine Source.

You probably have tons of questions, especially if you never considered yourself psychic. What it means is that you can sense information from the world around you. Everyone is capable of that. You might not understand how you receive it, because sometimes it seems to come from some magical place outside of you. It's as if stuff just pops in from the great beyond.

Since everyone has a sixth sense, you can experience life through non-physical senses as well as physical. You may be able to feel, see, taste, hear, smell, or know things that you won't always realize how.

The truth is that you can learn to understand this better. Let us focus on this in as simple terms as possible. Realize that being a psychic and accepting it is allowing yourself to receive guidance from a divine source. It's for your life's journey to be a successful one.

Let's face it; we are all human, we make mistakes, and we learn life lessons along the way. What's wonderful about realizing and utilizing our innate gifts is that we can learn to listen to our intuition to help us through challenging times. Life is a journey, and it has many ups and downs to help us evolve our soul.

Before we go any further, let's get something out in the open. Just because there are people that call themselves psychics and foretell futures for money, doesn't mean that you must do that. Plus, foretelling futures is not always possible in the way you might think. That's because we all have a free will regarding the choices we make. Meaning that we can do whatever we wish, and so can others around us. As an intuitive soul, learning to be a psychic and understanding your gifts, you may realize quickly that not everything is written in stone.

# Chapter 3
# Am I, Psychic

Sitting back, you may ask yourself how in the world you can be psychic, and if there is a way to tell quickly.

Does that sound like you? If so, let's find out. I'm going to list some common ways that psychic information can come through. If you can identify with anything, then realize you have experienced what being psychic is.

As you read through it, be aware that not every instance can be listed here. These are just examples. You probably have experienced things you would like to share and get feedback on. If that is the case, then I encourage you to join a class, read more books and find others who are on the same path and learning too.

## Exercise: Psychic Sample Test

Below are some common signs you might have experienced on an intuitive psychic level. Check off any that apply.

- ☐ Knowing who is on the other end when your phone rings or thinking of someone right before they ring.

- ☐ You are meeting a new person for the first time but feeling a magnetic pull and having the notion you have known the person forever or met them before.

- ☐ Having dreams of people, places, or things that you have never seen before but shortly after you do, and it feels like déjà vu.

- ☐ You know information about people that you don't know or have a sense that someone is lying.

- ☐ Seeing something occur in the future before it happens.

- ☐ You feel like your mind is continuously busy or experience white noise.

- ☐ You feel funny or uncomfortable in crowded spaces.

- ☐ You hear your name getting called and realize no one is there.

- ☐ You hear random music start playing in your ears, or you can't get a song out of your head.

- ☐ Feeling the physical pain or knowing when someone is not feeling well before they mention it.

- ☐ You get a heavy or worried feeling that something bad is about to happen before it does.

- ☐ You know what someone is going to say before they say it, or you can finish someone's sentence.

Look over the statements you checked off. Were there more or less than you expected? Remember, this is only a small sample, and most people don't think of it as being psychic. They assume it's a common feeling or coincidence and brush it off.

Many people have a lot of doubts or a misunderstanding because, in society, we get conditioned. I can tell you in classes when I ask students if the word psychic elicits a feeling of discomfort or doubt in them that almost all hands go up.

Are you able to say you are psychic without stuttering or having doubt? If so, don't worry. It can take time to understand, trust, and fully accept your intuition.

If, on the other hand, you have known that you are psychic, but haven't developed it, then perhaps you just need a little extra support to get on your path.

# *When I think of the word psychic, I feel?*

_____

_____

_____

_____

_____

_____

_____

_____

_____

_____

_____

_____

# Chapter 4
# Should I Be Fearful

This next subject was tough for me at the beginning of my journey during my awakening. I realize now that it was something I had to work through to be more empowered over my abilities.

You see, fear should never get tied into being psychic. The problem we have had over time is that people have labeled psychics as bad. The term made people feel uncomfortable and still does for some in society.

For many developing psychics or those people discovering their abilities, fear could force them to stop moving forward. You do not want to have doubts or worry over your natural gifts. You must learn to trust them. In time you will see that you are being protected, loved, and supported by the Divine and that nothing evil can harm you by using them for loving guidance.

Let's discuss it a little further. Some people say the word "psychic" is scary based upon some religions and beliefs. It's interesting to me that most people today can identify and think of themself as intuitive but not psychic. Truthfully, psychics are just intuitive people that have worked on their ability to increase their awareness and grow it to where they can trust it.

Either way, it's okay to think about what you will and use the terms that you are most comfortable with.  Know that it doesn't change that God, a Higher Power that created you, did so with the knowledge that to survive, you would need instincts. We call them survival instincts.

Cave dwellers had to go looking for food, shelter, and know how to stay alive once upon a time. They didn't have a GPS or an iPhone. They had their instinct to rely on.

Somewhere over time, our instincts have lessened, and we have grown dependent on other things to give us answers.

# Chapter 5

# Causes of Fear

## Fear of Being Wrong

Most people who don't choose to rely on their intuition is because they fear they will be wrong. They don't understand their natural ability is within them. It's there to help and guide on the journey through life if they wish to accept and trust it.

## Religious Perspectives

Some religions hold beliefs that those who consult with psychics are evil because they receive from a dark source. We know today, that is not the truth and more of an ancient perspective. People of faith are starting to realize that too and questioning the belief. There was a time where some aspects of certain religions were created by man to place control over society. One thing to consider if you are concerned with this is that in many religions, like Jesus and Mohammed, there was prophecy and spiritual healing phenomena.

## Fear of The Unknown

Some people still place a superstitious perspective upon it. They continue to view it as bad, mostly due to there being no real rational or scientific answers. Not everything is going to have an explanation, and that scares people. We truly must come to our realizations and truths on our journey.

## Charlatans and Frauds

There are people out there that have been practicing psychics and taking money from others with bad intentions. These people have given a poor reputation to being psychic. It might seem then that psychics are fraud and don't exist. In any job anywhere, there will always be people that are doing it for the wrong reasons and taking advantage of others. Perhaps due to these charlatans, a layer of skepticism forms that we must break free from.

## Afraid of What Others Will Think

Many people are scared to come out of the "psychic closet" for fear of what others will say. They worry people won't agree, especially in families and friendships where the others hold fearful views on psychics. They are afraid they might be looked at funny or called crazy or evil.

## The Blessing

Now that we have identified the fear let's see how being psychic and intuitive is a blessing and provides guidance from a loving source to help us.

*Example:*
Spouse says, "Honey, I have a bad feeling about us going out tonight driving in the rain."
Partner says, "Don't be silly. We will be fine."
But then, not even thirty minutes later they are in a car accident.

Perhaps if they had trusted the intuition, they might have stayed home safely. Some people brush it off as a coincidence, but sometimes the feeling has a reason. Learning to trust your intuition will help you realize the difference.

Let's look at another example of intuition. Only this time, intuition is realized and acted upon.

*Example:*
Spouse says, "Honey, turn the car around. I need to go to the store before dinner. I know we are hungry, but I feel we should go there first."
Partner Agrees, and thirty minutes later, they witness a pile up on the freeway with ambulances arriving. They quickly realize that if they had not stopped, they might have gotten involved.

So, you could say that was a guardian angel, and you would be right, but the angels giving the divine assistance came through using psychic intuition.

Sometimes we may have a quiet voice or feel something, and we realize we were saved or blessed. Other times, we may experience that we listen to our feelings only to see that nothing happens, or we don't get the results we desired. We may begin to think we can't trust our intuition. On the other hand, we might receive from our intuition and do the opposite only to be upset with ourselves later.

If this sounds familiar, know that you can change that. You can start to trust your inner guidance. When is that exactly you ask? When you start letting go of any fears and learning to believe it.  It takes patience and a willingness to be wrong sometimes. Yep, there will be occasions you will be mistaken, but that is okay. Over time, with patience and trust, it will evolve, and your senses will heighten. You will learn how to recognize instances where your intuition is speaking to you to guide you.

You will start to understand so much more. If you learn how your senses receive and what it means, you will slowly discover that you can have more control over what happens around you.

# Chapter 6
# Getting Started

I am going to share what I feel is helpful and straightforward when starting in developing your psychic senses. I will summarize this but go into more detail on some aspects in the next chapter.

The first step is to set your intention out to the universe. It will allow it to flow into all levels of your conscious mind that you want to connect and develop. Once you have done that, let yourself acknowledge and recognize that you are a psychic individual and that being psychic is a gift granted to all.

Release any fears and doubts that starting is wrong or harmful. Know that you are protected and loved by the Divine, God, and the Creator. Understand that we all have guides and angels wanting to help us move forward on our path for our highest and best.

Once you place out into the universe your desire to learn, you may begin to start seeing classes, teachers, new friends, books, and all kinds of information coming toward you. I encourage you to read and develop from more than one source. Everyone that has been down this path that may write, teach, or advise has something different that has worked for them.

We can all only share something for you to consider in your development. Things that we found helpful on our journey.

Know that anytime something is not working for you, that you can try another way. Sometimes things don't always work at the start, but down the line, they can. Release the worry that you will do anything wrong or learn something incorrectly. Much of what you will learn and how you learn it will be through practice and intuition.

If you need help, ask others for their advice and assistance. Not everyone will have the answers, but when you receive guidance, you will start to recognize what feels right and works best for you. Go with it. You can change thoughts, actions, or feelings later as you progress.

Another thing that is helpful when starting is allowing yourself the time to meditate daily. If you can't do it for 15-20 minutes a day, try to do it for five minutes and work up to 20 minutes. You can sit longer, use guided meditations, or sit quietly in your energy. Whatever method you choose to do, and wherever you decide to do it, it is up to you.

Many people feel early morning is best to meditate, while others do it at night. Some people find sitting in a chair and focusing on something is best, and yet others prefer to lie down and close their eyes. If you have questions about meditations, there are many great teachers and books available.

Learning to relax the mind through meditation will begin to help you to receive. It will quiet the outside noise of society and the everyday thoughts that can take over your mind and block you.

Once you understand the process of meditation and learn the psychic senses, then it's time to start to practice. On the following pages, I will provide you with essential information on the psychic senses so that you can understand how you receive on a psychic level. You can then start to learn and practice on your own doing simple exercises. You can also choose to find a partner that wishes to develop with you to practice. I will include some basic exercise ideas at the end of this book for you to get started.

# Chapter 7
# The Sixth Sense (Clairs)

We have our physical senses, and they are seeing, hearing, feeling, tasting, and smelling. When it comes to our sixth sense, we have those same senses but in a non-physical way. We can experience them from within us, and they are called Clairs.

Clairvoyance – Clear Seeing

Clairaudience – Clear Hearing

Clairsentience – Clear Feeling

Claircognizance – Clear Knowing

Clairgustance – Clear Tasting

Clairalience – Clear Smelling

These clairs can be present in everyone. However, from my experience, there will always be one or more of them that is stronger and will bring in more reliable information for you. These clairs can help you receive and provide you with messages, images, sounds, feelings, and impressions.

# Chapter 8
# What Are My Strongest Clairs

"Which clairs do I have?" That is one of the first questions often asked when people have identified that they are psychic. Students wish to know what to develop and how to grow. For my classes, I have created a short little list of questions and two different ways to help find the answer.

## Part I. Clairs Test

Ask yourself from the list below which statements you can identify with. Put a checkmark at each that applies to you.

### Clairvoyance

☐ I have a detailed and vivid recollection of things that happen.

☐ I sometimes see flashes of light, shadows, orbs, and images.

☐ I love looking at art, photographs, or going to museums.

☐ I daydream or dream vividly at night.

☐ I can easily see pictures and images with my eyes closed or open.

## Clairaudience

☐ I love music and often hear it in my head.

☐ I love listening to a great story, and I always lend an ear to a friend.

☐ I enjoy listening to the sounds of nature.

☐ I like to listen to the radio or podcasts.

☐ Sometimes I hear my name getting called, and no one is present.

## Claircognizance

☐ I know things sometimes instantly.

☐ I get lots of inspiration from out of the blue.

☐ I am always thinking of new ideas and enjoy writing.

☐ I sometimes know what others are thinking.

## Clairsentience

☐ I don't usually like crowded places as I feel strange.

☐ I sometimes know when others aren't feeling well physically or emotionally.

☐ I can feel when others are in pain on a physical level.

☐ I can walk in somewhere and feel the energy.

☐ Sometimes I can touch something and feel a vibration.

## Clairalience

☐ I can sometimes smell perfume when none is around.

☐ I can sometimes smell food before it gets cooked.

☐ I can smell what someone is eating from over the telephone or at a distance.

☐ When hearing a story, I can sometimes smell something relating to the story.

## Clairgustance

☐ I can sometimes taste the food that others have eaten.

☐ I sometimes get strange tastes in my mouth. i.e., smoke, tar, coal, etc.

☐ Sometimes I walk through the store and can taste something on a shelf without eating it.

☐ I can think of food and can taste a little of the flavor in my mouth.

Now that you have been able to complete the list, can you identify which clair(s) you checked off the most statements under? Let's try another exercise that looks at strength.

## CLAIRS STRENGTH TEST

### Clairvoyance – The Seeing Clair

When you are seeing, it's said to be with your third eye. This eye is right between the brows and works in connection with your pineal gland. Think of seeing with your third eye as being able to visualize and paint an image easily inside your mind.

### *Exercise 1: Clairvoyance*

To begin, you will close your eyes and take a couple of deep breaths doing your best to visualize white light around your body, encapsulating it.

Was that successful? _____

Next, try and think of someone that you talked to recently and close your eyes and see if you can visualize them. Take notice if you can see what they are wearing. Can you see any colors, or anything significant in detail?

Was that successful? _____

### *Exercise 2: Clairvoyance*

On a scale of 1 -5, on an average day, how easy is seeing in your mind, receiving visions, or daydreaming?

1. Impossible
2. Rare
3. Sometimes
4. Often
5. Always

## Clairaudience – The Hearing Clair

This clair is hearing, but it's not with your ears exactly. Most of this sense is heard from inside your head. You may be able to hold conversations in your mind. For instance, it could be a voice that gives you an answer back inside your head after you questioned something.

### Exercise 1: Clairaudience

1. Yes or No – Do you talk inside your head?

2. Yes or No – Do you hear an answer-back?

3. Yes or No - Does that voice say "You" rather than "I"?

4. Yes or No - Do you ever quickly hear a word or name in your head?

5. Yes or No – Does music get stuck or play in your head?

### Exercise 2: Clairaudience

On a scale of 1 -5, how often do you hear thoughts or phrases or music in your head?

1. Never
2. Rare
3. Sometimes
4. Often
5. Always

## Clairsentience – The Feeling Clair

This one I bet you can recognize, and you use almost every day to some varying degree depending on how sensitive you are. This clair is one of feeling. Many people that consider themselves empaths will relate. You might feel it emotionally, mentally, or physically.

### *Exercise 1: Clairsentience*

1.  Yes or No - Can you feel the energy when you walk into a room?

2.  Yes or No - Can you sense if the energy is good or bad feeling?

3.  Yes or No - Do you notice when someone is upset before they say it?

4.  Yes or No - Do you ever feel great and then suddenly feel different after you have been around someone angry, tired, or sad?

### *Exercise 2: Clairsentience*
On a scale of 1 -5, based on the questions above, how often does this happen, or do you notice it?

1.  Never
2.  Rare
3.  Sometimes
4.  Often
5.  Always

## Clairgustance – The Tasting Clair
This clair is tasting food or non-food items when you have not put it in your mouth.

### *Exercise 1: Clairgustance*

1.  Yes or No - Have you ever gotten a taste of something that you didn't eat?

2.  Yes or No – Have you ever tasted a food just thinking about it?

### *Exercise 2: Clairgustance*
On a scale of 1- 5, how often would you say that you experience tasting?

1. Never experienced
2. Rare
3. Sometimes
4. Often
5. Very

## Clairalience – The Smelling Clair
This clair is smelling scents that are not present.

### *Exercise 1: Clairalience*

1. Yes or No – Have you ever smelled perfume or smoke in a room where there was no perfume or smoke?

2. Yes or No – Have you ever smelled anything strange and questioned where it was coming from only to find no reason?

### *Exercise 2: Clairalience*
On a scale of 1- 5, how strong would you say that you experience these smells?

1. Never experienced
2. Rare
3. Sometimes
4. Often
5. Very

## Claircognizance – The Knowing Clair
This clair can be harder to detect. You may receive creative or inspiring ideas. You may also just know things at times instantly and not know why. It's like magical knowledge that just pops in.

### Exercise 1: Claircognizance

1. Yes or No – I always seem to know what to say to help people feel better.

2. Yes, or No – Words always flow out of my mouth, and I can write just the same.

3. Yes or No – Sometimes, I talk to my pets, and I know what they are thinking back to me.

### Exercise 2: Claircognizance
On a scale of 1- 5, how often does it happen where you just know stuff but can't explain how.

1. Never
2. Rare
3. Sometimes
4. Often
5. Always

Now that you finished these exercises, go back over them to see what stands out for you. Can you see where you identified with any specific clairs more easily? Can you see from Exercise #2 under each clair, which one was used more often and was strongest? Were you surprised?

Your stronger senses can help you receive and get guidance from the Divine. As you begin to practice and develop these senses, you will need to learn to trust the information. If you have other clairs that were also identified, but not as strong, know that you can develop them. In time, you can utilize the clairs and get them to work in harmony together. It will take time and practice, so be patient with yourself.

# EXERCISE: JOURNAL YOUR DEVELOPING CLAIRS

## Part I. My strongest psychic clairs are:
Write down which clairs you felt are strongest based on the results or your belief.

_____

_____

_____

_____

## Part II. My experiences with using my psychic clairs.
Sit quietly and recall when you may have experienced using your clairs and didn't realize it. Look back in six months and review this information to see your progress.

_____

_____

_____

_____

_____

# Chapter 9
# What Should I Consider

**Developing Your Intuition Takes Time and Patience**

I could say that ten thousand times, and I bet in your excitement, you would still feel eager and hopeful that it will happen overnight. I can say that even if you were a gifted psychic, with an ability to learn quickly, that you would still need to take steps to develop yourself.

I recognize that many newcomers tend to be impatient and desire to learn quickly. I know I did at the beginning. It was a process. Some people learning do pick up amazingly fast, but if there aren't stages to development, you will find that you are not receiving all that you could be. I believe that if you don't truly take the time to learn, you may get too much in your head. In which case, you won't be helping yourself. You may get led more by your ego. I have seen many psychics stop self-developing because they started and did just enough to get by.

## Psychic Blocks

Without proper development and self-care, you may feel blocks. Although we are all human, and it does happen to everyone from what I have witnessed. You may find it happens more often to you if you don't take time out for your personal development. You may struggle with receiving and not know what you can trust and rely on. It's then possible that you may begin using more of your conscious mind and your own opinions.

Through development, you are evolving your soul, realizing your true potential, seeing your path with more clarity, and healing yourself. The guidance granted to you seems unlimited. Why wouldn't you want to work hard to develop yourself? I feel you should make the most of what was divinely gifted to you to help with your soul's evolution. It will assist you in becoming a more peaceful, balanced, and happier person.

## Learning to Trust

Start trusting that little voice within you and what you feel. Sit in more silence and spend more time outdoors. Give your thoughts, feelings, or even small visions credit. The next time you think something, ask yourself why. Without thinking too hard, just take what comes to you. Let go and start to accept it, right or wrong.

Concentrate on what you got right every time. You will see that you will begin to get more and more correct. When that happens is different for everyone, so don't ever compare yourself with anyone else's progress. When you can learn to trust your natural ability, it will get stronger.

## Telling Yourself, You Are Psychic

Every day when you get up, you may want to create a positive statement. Maybe you already have encouraging words that keep you motivated and positive. If not, this may be a great time to put one together to help celebrate who you are and your abilities.

Create a simple statement that you can remember and say in the mirror or on your way to work, etc. It may help to reinforce your subconscious mind that you are genuinely psychic and happy being psychic!

## Learn to Ground Yourself

What is grounding? If you have already started down your path, you may have already heard of it. Some of you may wonder what it is. Grounding can help you feel more calm, relaxed, and centered during your psychic work. The benefits of grounding yourself include emotional and mental clarity. It will help with readings and in everyday life.

If you are newly awakening, you could have an excess of emotion and overwhelm. Some of that may or may not be your energy. As you go about your day, you want to be at peace and focused on increased awareness. You will find that meditating will be a huge stress reliever, which will improve your overall health in the end.

You should try to do your best to keep your body, mind, and soul at the most peaceful, relaxed state it can be to receive from the Divine. By grounding yourself, you are allowing that excess energy to have someplace to go. Grounding can be done in several ways because there is no right or wrong way if your intention is there.

Some people choose to visualize it, while others prefer to say it or go outside and walk in nature. You can go barefoot in the grass, garden, walk along the seashore, or simply sit quietly in your yard breathing in the fresh air.

If you are a visual person, you may want to try closing your eyes and seeing yourself standing on grass barefoot while cords come out of the bottoms of your feet and enter the earth's surface. Allow those cords to travel down for as far as you can see. Another visualization is imagining yourself as a large tree with roots extending down into Mother Earth.

If you would prefer to speak your intention, then put your intent out by stating an affirmation. Some people say the same statement each time, and some say a few quick words. Please do what you are comfortable with, as it is my experience that the universe will always comply.

## Meditation is Key

You may ask, why do I need to meditate anyway? Is that helpful? The answer is yes, as it helps you to learn how to quiet your mind. We go about our day-to-day lives, and we are so busy that we get caught up in many thoughts and emotions. When you learn to meditate, you are learning how to quiet the monkey mind. You are discovering how to shut out the external world with all the noise so that you can hear the quiet voice from within you. If you wish to receive using your senses, you will need to learn how to drown out all the noise and thoughts that keep your mind busy during the day.

## How to Properly Meditate

If there is one thing I express to people learning, it's that they don't need to put strict rules on how or when they meditate. Some people meditate daily and for hours at a time, while others do it when they have time. In my opinion, it doesn't matter where you meditate, so long as you find a way to give yourself time alone to sit in your power to just be at peace. Strive for daily or at least a few times a week. If a schedule is best for you and you desire to learn true meditation, then seek out books. There are many out there to help with this.

I have heard several people say they fall asleep, and, in my opinion, it's okay if you need sleep. Your body needs to relax and heal itself. You may be tired and drained. I also think that if you are trying to meditate at a particular time every day when you are tired that you should consider finding another time when you are more awake.

You can try meditation with or without sounds or guided music if that is easier. Some people sit and do breathing techniques. New people sometimes do better with guided meditations until they get more comfortable. Don't worry if you can't see anything or feel like you are not able to experience something during the meditation. The most important aspect is to sit quietly to try and clear your mind. Some people like to sit in nature and just listen to the sounds around them. You are being present in your surroundings and noticing the quiet and learning focus.

If you are concerned with not having time to meditate or can't seem to fit it into your schedule, then try it for short periods. Don't make it much longer than five minutes if that is the case. Try meditation little by little to learn to develop it. It's no different than setting aside time to go to the gym. You may not be able to last long during those first couple gym visits, but as you know, you will get stronger and better at it the more you do it.

Meditation will help you in the end, to relax the mind. Take your time, and don't give up.

## Taking Classes and Practicing with Others

If you can find a class, I encourage you to attend. I believe courses are a great help to beginners. However, it's up to you whether you wish to enroll in them. Often, you can find books in your local library or online for sale, along with free videos on YouTube.

Some websites provide access to small courses that are webinars. They may have groups that support you with access to the other students who have also enrolled. It is great because you can discuss your development and find others to practice with.

From my experience, it helps on your journey to meet other like-minded souls to share views and thoughts with. If you do not have anything in your area, look online for these classes, groups, communities, and schools to help. There are many great ones to try. You can ask for referrals, look at reviews, and just feel what is best for you when registering.

When searching around, if you don't like the energy or it feels like the wrong class, and you are insecure, then look for another. Try to find the best place for you to grow and learn in a non-judgmental and safe environment. Not all teachers or schools are the best fit for everyone. I will say, however, that you can learn something from everybody. Take what you need from each person, class, video, or book and move to the next one. You are a student for life, so stay focused and keep learning all that you can.

## Trusting Your Intuition

Did you know that even the most noted psychics in the world are not 100% accurate? No one is perfect. Receiving messages and interpreting impressions is not the same for everyone. We are all different and must practice to learn. The more we work with our ability, the more clearly, we will begin to see how our mind receives from the Divine. Remember that working on a psychic level is not an exact science.

I think sometimes people may believe that if they read a certain book or take the right class with the best instructor that the lights will come on. They think they will be a professional psychic or a psychic medium overnight. Though some people can pick it up faster than others, there is no special pill to swallow or words to say to make it happen quickly.

I have said it before in this book and will repeat it. You must practice, have patience, and accept that everything will happen in the time it is supposed to for you. Don't race your development. Sit with what you receive and keep practicing to understand and improve. Eventually, you will have a better grasp of what is coming to you.

## Don't Use Your Thinking Mind

When trying to receive information psychically, you want to be careful that you don't get caught up in using your mind to interpret the impressions. From the time we are little, we are molded and taught to think. We are told to take something and sit with it to learn and grasp it through analyzing. When doing work with your psyche, that process disrupts, lessens, and weakens your ability.

What you should consider instead is to allow yourself the freedom to speak spontaneously, letting go of your conscious mind's need to attach itself to everything that comes into your head. When you get an image, word, feeling, thought, or hear something, don't allow yourself to have an opinion. Focus on letting yourself receive additional information instead of stopping to think about it.

Questioning anything should only be answered by receiving more and not by you figuring it out. I know that sounds difficult because you must unlearn what you have always been taught to do when you don't understand something.

Some people try to learn symbols from books. They aim to memorize them to understand and train themselves with what they are receiving to know what is coming in. I think if you are practicing a lot and have determined time and time again that what you receive has a specific meaning, then you are learning how to work with your ability.

If, however, you are using symbol books to train yourself, be cautious that you don't learn something and need to place thinking upon it during your reading. The information should flow, and more practice will help you grow.

If you need to understand anything, because you are struggling, then consider doing it later when you can sit in a quiet place alone with your guides. Ask them questions regarding what you got and then, let go of needing a direct answer. Simply allow them to provide you with more information and in a different way that you can understand better.

When it comes to your intuition, realize that information should travel toward you. Don't look for anything or reach for it. That is your ego and thinking mind trying to interfere. It sounds painful, and sometimes it feels exhausting. If that is the case, stop and try again later. Give yourself time.

Sometimes, in your practice and development, you just need to step back when you feel frustrated or aren't seeming to have a connection. Let yourself take a deep breath to calm your mind. Tell your brain and body to release and let go. Remind yourself you are safe, and all is well. Acknowledge that you are naturally psychic and will learn how to use your intuition. When you do start to receive, bring in everything and don't think about anything. Don't assume it's crazy, foolish, stupid, unrelatable, or will hold no value. Just because you might get something that doesn't make sense immediately, doesn't mean that it's not credible and can't get validated in some way.

When you start to accept what you are receiving, there will be messages sent to your psychic brain telling it that you respect what it has to say. In other words, you are showing your intuition that you wish to start using it more because you appreciate its worth. Your psychic mind will then know you are deciding to develop. It helps you set your intention to take your skills to the next level.

While you might be thinking it won't ever happen, just tell yourself that it will. Over time, what might be one word, one small feeling or thought, will change to another and another, and soon you will hold longer links and get more information on a psychic level.

## Know That You Are Not Alone

As you start to awaken your psychic ability, you may go through a series of mixed emotions in your development. It may come in stages, and you will see over time who and what in your life needs to fall away will.  The best advice I can give you is that you are never alone.  As you are learning to trust in yourself and the universe, you will start to recognize that.

Sometimes the people in our lives won't always understand or accept the decisions and choices we make, but it's not their life. You need to do what is right for you at every stage of your development. Release, surrender, and let go of others and their opinions of you with love. Don't allow others to control what brings you joy as we all have a right to be happy and at peace.

If you feel like you are losing friends, know that there are many great communities full of people that have gone through the same thing. They understand and accept these God-given gifts.

You may not be ready to release those around you, but you can forgive them and yourself for any hard feelings. Allow others to shift in the time they are supposed to. You can't change people, but you don't have to allow them to try and change you either.  Everyone must find their place in time with their spirituality.

If you are setting the intention to find others, they will come when you are ready. Again, I repeat that you are not alone, and the Spirit world is all around you and supporting you in your new endeavors. You may not always feel their love and support, but in time as you grow, you will most likely start to see things differently.

## Spirit Guides

I want to mention that it is my belief, like many others, that we have guides and angels that help us. It's my experience that we have at least one with us throughout our lives and others that come and go. These guides are providing us with whatever assistance we need at the time to make our path more successful. If you want to know more about them, find a great book on spirit guides, or look online.

If you ever wish to try meeting your spirit guides, try sitting quietly and meditating after setting an intention in your mind or out loud to meet them. You may see them, hear them, feel them, or just know they are. Don't get upset if this takes a while or even years.

You might listen to some people that have met their guides and have names, dates, and information describing what their guides look like. Don't get caught up in this and worry you have done anything wrong if you don't receive the same. It doesn't mean you are alone or don't have guides. It might mean the timing isn't best. Be patient, even when you are sick of being patient! Instead, use whatever experiences you have as lessons and opportunities to grow and develop trust.

## Positive Mindset

I can't tell you how important it is to be positive. You are human, and no doubt, you will have days that you are tired, cranky, frustrated, or even mad. It's okay to get upset but learn to adopt a positive mindset as you go about your days. You will be surprised how merely saying something loving to yourself or others will make you feel. It will help to raise your vibration, and having a higher vibration is so vital, in my opinion, when working with your psychic ability.

You are helping your body, mind, and soul to radiate peace and joy. When you are happy, you are more relaxed, inspired, and brighter. You want to be lighter and calmer, so work on smiling and putting out happy thoughts.

At first, it may be hard, but over time, it should get more comfortable. In my own life, I know that I had days where I was in a low place, and when I would practice putting out happy thoughts to the universe, it felt fake. I thought I was trying to deceive myself. However, over time, I noticed that as I went about my day with loving affirmations and reminders, that it got easier. Soon, I felt lighter, and I didn't have to convince myself. I'm not saying that I don't still have days, but once I learned, I trusted and knew that it would pass, and brighter days would return.

## Love Yourself

Yep, I said it. You need to love and look at yourself as a healthy and loving soul. You have been brought down into a physical body to experience, learn, and grow. Above all things, to learn about love. That includes loving others, the universe, the earth, and all the elements and animals on the planet. Most importantly, is that you need to learn to love yourself and release judgments. You are wonderful, unique, and perfect in every way.

If you feel anything but love, then you are living with fear. Don't be consumed by your shadow self or ego. We all have an ego, and it can be used to motivate us positively, but it shouldn't be allowed to slow us down or halt us.

You need to understand that you are human and having a human experience. You won't always be right or do the right things. You will make mistakes, and that is okay, but you need to release the idea that you must be perfect.

I know many people that strive for perfection. I did too for a while and had to release that tendency. Let me tell you that it can create issues. If you are operating as a perfectionist, you are overly concerned with how others perceive you or how you see yourself. If you are too hard on yourself, know now that is your ego, and you need to tell it to step aside. You are doing excellent work, and no matter your progress; you are going upward. It may take you a while, but the more you release the judgments and learn to love yourself for who you are, the better and farther you will go.

## A Tip When Practicing

Remember, as you are practicing in the beginning, that what you receive and validate may start minimally. You may get frustrated but surrender to the process. Let go of what was wrong or what you didn't understand. Don't beat yourself up. Concentrate on what you got right, and more will follow with patience.

As you do this, you will find over time that your trust in yourself will also develop. When you learn to trust in your ability, the doors will open further.

Lastly, don't ever tell yourself that you can't do it or that you are not psychic. You want to use positive affirmations even more in my opinion during those times that your ego comes in with doubts. I encourage you to remind yourself how far you have come and how well you are doing. Keep positive, and enjoy your new journey.

# Chapter 10

# The Basics Summary

These are the things to keep in mind on your journey forward with your psychic development.

- Surrender
- Let go of wanting to think
- Be okay with being wrong
- Have patience
- Drink plenty of water and eat healthful foods
- Take care of your body and get regular exercise
- Find out what psychic clairs are your strongest
- Trust in yourself and the Divine
- Practice alone or with a partner
- Read or watch videos on development
- Learn how to forgive yourself and others
- Release fears and judgments
- Tell yourself today, "I Am Psychic."
- Believe in yourself
- Know you are not alone
- Love yourself
- Ground yourself

- Meditate daily if possible
- Practice with a partner
- Keep a positive mindset
- Join an online or local class or practice circle

## Tips on Receiving

- Set your intention to ground and center yourself.
- Call out to your guides for their assistance.
- Ask for loving white light to surround you.
- Take some deep breaths and exhale fully, letting go of thoughts.
- Tell your mind it's time to receive only from the Divine.
- Receiving can come in through one clair or more of them.
- Sometimes your clairs will work one at a time or simultaneously.
- You may notice a feeling, whether it's a physical sensation that comes on slowly or an emotion.
- You may see colors, full or partial images, movie clips, flashes of light, or symbols, etc.
- You may hear sounds, voices, a word, sentence, or a song, etc.
- You may have a sudden knowing of information or a thought.
- You may smell or taste something.
- Note whatever you are getting and don't think it crazy.

# Practice and Exercises

Exercise ideas are in this book for you to work on either alone or with a partner. If you are looking for more ideas, you could try searching online or getting books that focus solely on psychic exercises to grow your intuition.

**Exercise 1.**

Find something in your home that you own, like a piece of jewelry or an ornament of some kind, and sit with it quietly to receive impressions, sounds, feelings, thoughts, images, etc. Because you know about the item, this exercise is not for anything other than to help you release your mind from wanting to take control. It is about you just receiving what is coming to you and making notes on how it is coming in. Jot down what you receive after you are done and then look it over.

The object I used was:

_____

When I held the object, I received messages through the use of my clairs—list which ones.

_____

_____

The impressions I received:

_____

_____

_____

_____

_____

_____

_____

_____

_____

_____

_____

## Exercise 2:

Find an heirloom in your home and hold it to receive impressions.

The object I used was:

_____

When I held the object, I received messages using my clairs. List which ones you felt you received from.

_____

_____

_____

The impressions I received:

_____

_____

_____

_____

_____

_____

_____

_____

## Exercise 3:

Sit quietly in a chair with a photograph in your hand. Looking at the picture, close your eyes and then paint that image inside your mind. See it with as much detail as you can and hold it. Allow yourself to receive more about that photograph, if possible. Try to pick up what happened the day the picture was taken. See what comes in through your clairvoyance or even your other senses.

Detail your experience below about what you received and what it meant to you.

_____

_____

_____

_____

_____

_____

_____

_____

## Exercise 4.

Sit on a chair with a lit candle at a nearby table that you can focus on. Clearing your mind, focus on just the light of the candle, and let your mind travel. Let go completely and just sit quietly for as long as you can.

Detail your experience below about what you received. How did it feel to focus on the light of the candle? Was it easy or difficult?

## Exercise 5:

Go outside early in the morning and sit quietly somewhere and allow yourself to listen to the sounds all around your neighborhood. Calming and clearing your mind, don't let it drift off. Just focus on your breathing and the sounds around you.

Journal your experience of being outside focusing and discuss what you heard and if you noticed new sounds that you don't usually pick up on. When you were through, how did you feel?

_____

_____

_____

_____

_____

_____

_____

_____

_____

_____

_____

_____

## Exercise 6:

Find a pack of cards and turn 5 of them face down. Using your intuition, see if you can pick up the color, number, image, or symbol of the card. Write down what you are receiving.

Card 1: _____

Card 2: _____

Card 3: _____

Card 4: _____

Card 5: _____

Turn the cards over and examine what you received right and note your experience below.

_____

_____

_____

_____

_____

_____

_____

Try this exercise again; only this time, try doing it a couple of different ways.

- Try going through the deck and focusing on receiving insight from your strongest clair.
- Try focusing only on color.
- Try focusing only on the symbol.

## Exercise 7:

Make yourself Zener cards, like the ones used in ESP to practice with. Get some paper or index cards to make the following symbols. You can then practice receiving with them on your own.

There are also websites online that offer free Zener card games to work with. If you have a partner to practice with, have them hold the cards and send them to you telepathically. They can visualize them or hold them up, but you want them to concentrate with you while you are trying to receive impressions.

## Exercise 8:

Grab a partner to join you in sending you telepathic messages. They can send you an image, thought, word, or number for you to try and pick up on.

## Exercise 9:

Have someone hide a small object in your home. Sit quietly and receive all that you can for where that object may be hidden. Notice the furniture, colors, room, etc. Try to pick up everything to see if you can find where it was placed.

**Exercise 10:**
Whenever the phone rings or a text sounds off, don't look right away at the caller ID. See if you can think of who is calling first.

**Exercise 11:**
The night before you go to bed, ask yourself who will be the first random person to call you the next day and at what time they will call. See if you get any impressions. Maybe you will even pick up what some of the conversation will be about.

**Exercise 12:**
See if you can guess whose email will come through first for the next day. Then see if you can receive how many emails you will bring in all day long.

**Exercise 13:**
If you have vivid dreams, get a dream journal, and keep it by your bed—every morning, document what you received. Dreams often have meaning. There are many dream books for sale to help you understand them if you are curious.

**Exercise 14:**
Think of a question you wish to ask your guides for help with. Take a couple of deep breaths. Clear your mind and set your intention to receive guidance. Close your eyes and allow yourself to receive everything that you can and write it down. If you wish to write down what you are hearing, feeling, or knowing during it, try that. Sometimes people receive through inspirational writing. Just let go and release and receive.

_____

_____

_____

_____

## Exercise 15:

Take out a canned item of food from your pantry. Sit it next to you. Concentrating on the food in the can, see if you can receive impressions, primarily through taste or smell.

What was your experience?

_____

_____

_____

_____

_____

## Exercise 16:

Write down three positive affirmations that you can use to help your psychic development. Example: I am grateful, loving, and psychic.

_____

_____

_____

_____

_____

_____

## Exercise 17:
Have a friend put a small object in a box. Set the box in front of you and allow yourself to receive what is inside. If your friend is not near you, have them focus on an object in their home and send you telepathically the object for you to pick up impressions.

## Exercise 18:
See if a friend will allow you to pick up things about their day. Allow yourself to share whatever you receive.

## Exercise 19:
Before you leave for work, school, or to go to the store, see if you can ask about the type of car that you will drive behind. Ask for color, name, license plate, and any details.

## Exercise 20:
The next time you have to go shopping, ask where your parking spot will be in terms of the row, space, and even what cars you will be parked next to.

Printed in Great Britain
by Amazon

85922465R00036